WHAT IT MEANS TO
BE A
CHURCH LEADER
A Biblical Point of View

WHAT IT MEANS TO BE A CHURCH LEADER:
A BIBLICAL POINT OF VIEW

Copyright © 1984 by Spiritual Growth Resources

Library of Congress Cataloging in Publication Data

NORMAN SHAWCHUCK
What It Means To Be A Church Leader: A Biblical Point of View
Bibliography: p.
1. Christian leadership.   I. Shawchuck, Norman, 1935

ISBN 0-938-180-13-4

Scripture quotations noted RSV are from the Revised Standard Version Common Bible, copyrighted © 1973, by the Division of Christian Education of the National Council of the Churches of Christ in the U.S.A., and used by permission.

The scripture quotation noted NASB is from the American Standard Bible, © the Lockman Foundation 1960, 1962, 1963, 1968, 1971, 1972,1973, 1975.

PRINTED IN THE UNITED STATES OF AMERICA

TABLE OF CONTENTS

PREFACE

I have written this book to tell you what I understand to be the purposes and behavioral expressions of ministry to the church. I have attempted to say all of this in a way that might inform and influence your own understanding and behavior as one called by God to lead his people.

Having said all this, I want to tell you that the single most important principle for each of us must be that the effective Christian leader of today must still be what he/she has always had to be — a person of prayer. For too long we have been trying to ignore and deny this — we can do so no longer. If our ministries, whether priest, prophet, or leader, are not built upon a life of prayer our best, most noble efforts will ultimately come to emptiness (Ps. 127:1,2).

I have counselled hundreds of pastors who have tried to build a ministry upon foundations of hard work, education, charisma, politics, popularity. I can tell you it doesn't work! de Foucauld said, "the soul will bring forth fruits exactly in the measure in which the inner life is developed in it. If there is no inner life, however great may be the zeal, the high intention, the hard work, no fruit will come forth . . .[1]

We were never told to counsel always, to preach always, to organize always; we are told to pray always. Bonhoeffer said the highest form of ministry we have to offer the church and the world is, after all, the ministry of intercessory prayer.[2] Deep down inside I know these men are correct.

FOOTNOTES: Preface

1. Charles de Foucauld, *Meditations of A Hermit,* trans. by Charlotte Balfour, Orbis, 1981.

2. Dietterich Bonhoeffer, *Life Together,* Harper & Row, 1954.

MINISTERS ARE . . .   like

TRUMPETS —
    which make no sound if
    breath be not breathed in them.   or like Ezekiel's

WHEELS —
    which move but not unless
    the Spirit moves them.   or like Elisha's

SERVANTS —
    whose presence does no good
    unless Elisha's spirit be there also.

— John Flavel

"I tell you the truth, the man who does not enter the sheep pen by the gate, but climbs in by some other way, is a thief and a robber. The man who enters by the gate is the shepherd of his sheep. The watchman opens the gate for him, and the sheep listen to his voice. He calls his own sheep by name and leads them out. When he has brought out all his own, he goes on ahead of them, and his sheep follow him because they know his voice. But they will never follow a stranger; in fact, they will run away from him because they do not recognize a stranger's voice."

John 10:1-5

"Jesus called them together and said, "You know that those who are regarded as rulers of the Gentiles lord it over them, and their high officials exercise authority over them. Not so with you. Instead, whoever wants to become great among you must be your servant, and whoever wants to be first must be slave of all. For even the Son of Man did not come to be served, but to serve, and to give his life as a ransom for many.' "

Mark 10:42-45

11

THE BIBLICAL PATTERN OF
LEADERSHIP FOR THE CHURCH

Christ introduced two ministry models to which an effective church leader must give himself or herself. For Jesus these were not merely abstract concepts, they were absolute standards for leadership behavior. The models are the Good Shepherd and the servant-leader.

THE GOOD SHEPHERD: John 10:1-18

The figure of the Good Shepherd[1], so loved and so often misunderstood, makes it clear that the calling and responsibility of the pastor includes both that of the "priest" and of the "leader."

The Pastor as "Priest"
The Good Shepherd, Jesus said, calls the sheep each by name. Many pastors today do not know their people by their names. They know them by the committees they lead, by the amount they contribute, by the work they do. They know them not as individual persons, but as supporters, or workers, or new members, or opponents. In such cases the relationship is not that of a shepherd.

When you call a person by name, that means you care for them as persons. You know them for who they are, not alone for what they do. This is essential to the relationship of a shepherd with the people.

The Shepherd as "Leader"
The Good Shepherd, Jesus said, not only calls the sheep by name, but also "leads them out" from the comfort

and security of the sheepfold into the world outside. The Good Shepherd is not only their priest who know them, each one, by name, but also their leader, whom they follow because they know his voice. They trust him and know he will go with them.

We have so sentimentalized the image of the Good Shepherd that the picture which comes to our mind is the shepherd, on the front of a children's Bible story book, in a green meadow, with little lambs frolicing about. But that is not the image of the shepherd in Scripture. Ezekiel protrays the shepherd as a warrior and judge, see chapter 34. David models an image of the ideal shepherd; a protector, a warrior, a king doing justice, protecting the congregation in warfare and peace.

The image of "king" has little meaning in our world, but our word "leader" comes very close to matching the "king" of the Old Testament. This is what Jesus had in mind when he said, "and (he) leads them out."

There is an important ministry which comforts and consoles the people, a ministry which knows persons for whom they are, not for the work they do. This is only half of the shepherd's job; however. The other half is to lead them out of their little security systems into the awesome task of establishing the kingdom of God upon earth.

Persons are known by their names, but also by their actions, Mt. 25:1-46. The priest and the leader are both reflections of the Good Shepherd who offers the people all of the ministry God wants them to have.

THE SERVANT-LEADER: Mark 10:42-45

One day Jesus was teaching his disciples, "The Son of Man is to be delivered up into the hands of men, and they will kill him; and when he has been killed he will rise again three days later." But they did not understand this and immediately began arguing about which of them would be the greatest in the new kingdom. He sat down and called them to him and said, "If anyone wants to be first he shall be last of all, and servant of all," Mark 9:31-35.

Jesus certainly had his leadership problems!

He often found it quite impossible to keep his disciples in good relationships with one another—and working together to accomplish his mission in the world. No matter how hard he tried to explain it, they never could understand, they never could envision the kingdom he described. He spoke of the kingdom of God. They could only envision a human kingdom in which they would rule. Even at the Last Supper they were still arguing over who would be "top dog," Lk. 22:24. He literally had to die before they understood. Up until the very last they were still denying him, betraying him, complaining because he hadn't carried out HIS mission exactly as THEY wanted him to, Luke 24:21.

Does this sound familiar? Do persons with whom you work ever misunderstand your leadership? Do they complain because you don't meet their expectations? Do they argue over who should have the right to make the decisions?

On another occasion the disciples were once again arguing over who deserved to be the greatest among them. In studying Jesus' response to them we gain insight into his own understanding of leadership for the church.

A dispute also arose among them, which of them was to be regarded as the greatest. And calling them to Himself, Jesus said to them, "You know that those who are recognized as rulers of the Gentiles lord it over them; and their great men exercise authority over them. But it is not so among you, but whoever wishes to become great among you shall be your servant; and whoever wishes to be first among you shall be slave of all. For even the Son of Man did not come to be served, but to serve, and to give His life a ransom for many," Mark 10:42-45.

Nothing is clearer in our Lord's teaching than his opinion that leadership among his people is not to be modeled on the pattern of leadership in the world. The prevailing world pattern of leadership is control, to dictate, to boss by power and authority. The simple word of Jesus is, "it shall not be so among you." We must not allow the

14

world's patterns of leadership to predominate in the church.

Even the people and institutions of the world are finding the old pattern intolerable. All over the world the old authoritarian pattern is being challenged - and in America authoritarian leadership is dead! Everywhere people are demanding more participation in the decisions which effect their lives. This, however, should not greatly worry leaders in the church, for Christ never intended this to be the church's leadership pattern.

Indeed, Christ's teachings and model of leadership can be summed up in a word: "Let the greatest among you become a servant . . . I am among you as one who serves." Jesus advocated servant-leadership.

Jesus simply said the effective leader must want to be a servant first. Deep down inside the leader must want to lead in order to serve. Leadership is for the people, not for the leader. The leader must live to serve the people, not vice versa. The leader must be a servant-leader[2], one who serves the people by and through his/her leadership.

Such a leader will never be short of followers. People will always respond to a leader who is first proven and trusted as a servant.

By word and example Jesus drew for us a clear picture of the quality and type of leadership he wants for the church. He taught first of all that leadership in the church is not to be modeled after secular patterns.

He also taught that the leader must have more than one behavioral style. The pastor must be both "priest" and "leader." All who wish to guide and influence the church must be both "servant" and "leader."

In addition to priest and leader, Jesus modeled another ministry style; that of prophet. These three comprise the patterns of ministry Jesus left for the church.

In addition, Jesus consistently modeled three types of interpersonal relationships; affirmation, challenge, separation. When you once understand this, you will see that Jesus gave us a clear picture of how a leader might best influence the attitudes and behaviors of persons.

When he first met someone he demonstrated acceptance and affirmation. Then as the person began to trust his concern for their well-being, he would begin to challenge those attitudes or behaviors which he felt were damaging to the person's own wholeness. After he knew both his concern and his challenge were understood, he would leave the person alone for a while to give him/her the freedom to decide how he/she wished to respond to the challenge.

We can chart his "leadership theory" in action.

The story of the woman caught in adultery, John 8:1-11, is a good example:

Affirmation: When the lawyers drug this woman to Jesus in the Temple, you can be certain she wasn't feeling very good about herself. She was feeling unaffirmed and unacceptable.

But Jesus soon let her know she was acceptable to him, and no worse than anyone else in the crowd. Probably the most affirming words she had ever heard were, "neither do I condemn you . . ."

Challenge: I think he looked into her eyes for a spark of recognition that he loved her just as she was, and as soon as he knew she felt his love he challenged the behavior that got her in trouble in the first place, "sin no more." He wanted her to know she need not continue her life style. He wanted her to know that even though he accepted her as she was, she need not stay as she was.

Separation: Than he told her in a single word that he trusted her to have the maturity and desire she needed to better her life, "Go!" In that single word he told her, "you don't need me checking up on you every minute to see whether you are living up to my expectations. I believe you will on your own. You are free to go now to make a new life for yourself."

The story of the two disciples on the road to Emmaus, Luke 24:13-31, offers another example:

Affirmation: When Jesus came to walk with them they weren't feeling too affirmed. In fact, as he joined them, "they stood still, their faces downcast," v. 17. But he soon had them telling their story—and knowing that he deeply cared for them.

Challenge: After a while he began to challenge their ideas about what had happened. "How foolish you are, and how slow of heart to believe . . ."

Separation: When once they were at their home they invited him in and he sat down to eat with them. He affirmed them and their home with his gracious presence, and in this they recognized who he was. Immediately he disappeared from their sight, v. 31.

This wasn't a separation which said, "I don't accept you. I don't want to be with you. So I'm leaving." It was a separation that communicated, "Now that you know I'm alive, I trust you to do what's right." They got the message — and acted on it, vv. 33-35.

What is the intent of Jesus' acting this way with persons? What is he trying to teach us about our own leadership? He is teaching us that sometimes we must be "priest"; we must accept, affirm, forgive, love the people whom we wish to influence and lead. At other times we must be "prophet"; we must challenge, confront, instruct, disagree. And on other occasions we must be "leader"; we must help them set goals, make plans, marshal resources and create programs to change their lives and world. Then we must give them the freedom to carry out their plans, to succeed, to fail, to learn. For by this they grow from immature, weak Christians who stumble over every stone, or collapse under every adversity, into strong Christians who are quite capable of serving God in every circumstance.

The pattern of leadership which Christ modeled was, in fact, born in the experience of the congregation in the Old Testament. The next chapter will discuss the types of ministry in the Old Testament.

17

FOOTNOTES: The Biblical Pattern of Leadership for the Church

1. This section is much influenced by my reading of the book *The Good Shepherd*, Lesslie Newbigin, Eerdmans Publishing Co., 1977.
2. The concept of servant-leader is discussed in depth by Robert Greenleaf in *Servant-Leadership*, Paulist Press, 1977.

This space is reserved for you to jot down your learnings and to add your own thoughts to the chapter.

THE THREE TYPES OF MINISTRY
IN THE OLD TESTAMENT

There were three types of leadership ministries offered to the congregation of Israel: that of the priest, the prophet, and the king. This was not always so. At first, when the tribe was very young and small it was led by family chiefs. Later certain "Judges" emerged to lead them. Finally as the tribe grew, divided into more separate units, became more complex, it became necessary for leadership to become more formalized and distinct.

Leadership came to be offered by three "offices": The priest, prophet, and king. They were each distinct; the priest was not the prophet, the prophet was not the king and the king was neither of the other two. They were, however, very much related to each other. The effectiveness of each one depended upon the response and cooperation of the other two. All three ministries were going on in the congregation at the same time, being carried out by different persons.

The three ministries were very different in character and intent, but they were all of equal importance:

The priest cared for the temple worship, provided for the sacrifices, forgave sins, announced pardon, comforted the people.

The prophet stressed the need for a social expression of the congregation's interior faith in acts of truth, love and justice; convinced of sin; announced judgment, dis-comforted the people.

The king managed the temporal affairs of the congregation; made decisions, settled arguments, solved problems, provided for necessary programs and policies to govern their life together, offered protection from foreign enemies.

The functions of the three were not quite as cleanly separated as I have described them. There was some overlap. Nonetheless, they were always distinct enough that the people had no difficulty knowing who was the priest, who was the prophet and who was the king.

The priest ministered primarily to the needs of persons within the context of the congregation. The prophet spoke primarily to the congregation as a whole. And the king ministered primarily to the corporate structures which governed the lives of the people.

The overall ministry to the Old Testament congregation would have been severely crippled had any one of the three expressions of ministry been lacking. Had there been only a prophet to convict the people of their sins but no priest to point the way to forgiveness, had there been only a priest to care for spiritual affairs but no king to manage temporal affairs, it's likely the congregation never would have possessed its promised land.

These three ministries were carried into the New Testament to become the models for ministry for every church in every generation. The next chapter will discuss the New Testament model for these ministries.

This space is reserved for you to jot down your learnings and to add your own thoughts to the chapter.

"Therefore, since we have a great high priest who has gone through the heavens, Jesus the Son of God, let us hold firmly to the faith we profess. For we do not have a high priest who is unable to sympathize with our weaknesses, but we have one who has been tempted in every way, just as we are—yet was without sin. Let us then approach the throne of grace with confidence, so that we may receive mercy and find grace to help us in our time of need."

Hebrews 4:14-16

"For Moses said, 'The Lord your God will raise up for you a prophet like me from among your own people; you must listen to everything he tells you. Anyone who does not listen to him will be completely cut off from among his people.' "

"When God raised up his servant, he sent him first to you to bless you by turning each of you from your wicked ways."

Acts 3:22,23 and 26

"For to us a child is born, to us a son is given, and the government will be on his shoulders. And he will be called Wonderful Counselor, Mighty God, Everlasting Father, Prince of Peace. Of the increase of his government and peace there will be no end. He will reign on David's throne and over his kingdom, establishing and upholding it with justice and righteousness from that time on and forever. The zeal of the Lord Almighty will accomplish this."

Isaiah 9:6,7

THE THREE-IN-ONE MINISTRY TO
THE NEW TESTAMENT CHURCH

THE THREE-IN-ONE MINISTRY OF CHRIST

The uniqueness of the ministry of Christ is that he gathered the three ministries into one person; so that he became our priest, our prophet, and our king. He did not "melt" the three ministries into one. He did not destroy their individual distinctiveness. He simply as one person embodied all three ministries.

THE UNIQUE CALL TO ALL PASTORS
AND SHEPHERDS OF THE CHURCH

From the beginning of the New Testament Church God has continued to provide the three-in-one ministry to congregations through the calling of pastors. The pastor's ministry is unique from all other ministries. Christ chooses to hold the pastor uniquely responsible to see to it that all three ministries are given equal emphasis and effectiveness within the local church. THE PASTOR NEED NOT, IN FACT IN MOST INSTANCES CAN NOT, DO ALL THREE ALONE—BUT MUST SEE TO IT THAT ALL THREE ARE OPERATING WITHIN THE CONGRE-GATION. The pastor CAN and SHOULD delegate aspects of the three ministries to others, but the pastor cannot delegate the responsibility for seeing they are each being carried out.

In carrying out this responsibility it is necessary for the pastor to recruit other leaders, lay or clergy, to serve within the three-in-one ministry, to see to it that they are properly

24

trained and resourced to ensure their effectiveness[1]. Paul refers to this responsibility in Eph. 4:11-16, "And He gave some as . . . pastors and teachers, for the equipping of the saints for the work of service to the building up of the body of Christ," vv. 11, 12.

We can illustrate the three types of ministry God has chosen to provide his congregation as follows:

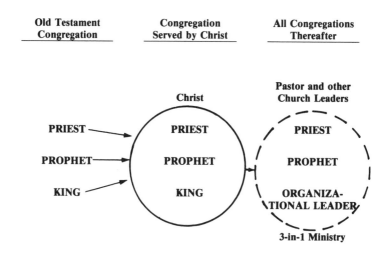

A SPECIAL WORD ABOUT THE MINISTRY OF ORGANIZATIONAL LEADERSHIP

God's grace is poured upon corporate human enterprise (organization) as well as upon individual members who happen to be involved in that enterprise. Corporate disciplines and programs in the church; such as planning, organizing, and delegating work; program ministries such as Sunday School, choir, social concerns; all of these are rooted in a belief that God works through these disciplines and organizations, just as he does through individuals.

There are many ministries which cannot be accomplished by an individual, nor by a number of individuals each working in his or her own way. Many of the greater minis-

25

tries depend upon a group of persons who pool their energies and resourcs, and organize their activities toward a single goal. Whenever people do this an amazing thing happens; the energy generated by the people working together is always greater than the energy generated by the persons each working alone. There is something very real to Jesus' word that where two or three are *together*, he is also there. The Spirit of Jesus is the "extra ingredient" added in Christian organization.

God knew this. That is why he provided for ministry to organizations as well as the ministry of prophetic word and of priestly care, but the ministry of caring for the organizations of the church has fallen into disrepute in many circles. "Administration" sounds too boring, and "management" sounds too secular.

Yet the truth is, the word "management" when it is exercised by responsible, caring persons, has an almost exact corollary in the New Testament. That word is "stewardship." Christian stewardship has always related to management. For the individual it has always involved the management of one's time, talent, and treasure. At the organizational level it involves the management of the congregation's collective time, talent and treasure.

There is another important corollary between management and stewardship. A manager manages on behalf of, and is accountable to an owner(s). A steward manages on behalf of, and is accountable to a master. We are given insight into the same meaning of the two words in Jesus' parable in Luke 19:11-27. In verse 13 the master is found saying to his stewards, "Do business with these (properties and budgets) until I come back." Doing "business" with organizations, budgets, and workers was the ministry of the Old Testament king, and of the New Testament steward; and is the business of today's pastor-as-organizational leader (manager).

The pastor is the primary organizational steward of the local church (this is a stewardship shared with other lay and clergy leaders) and as such is accountable to Christ as Lord of the Church, and to the church as one of its servant-leaders. The pastor must carry a sense of accountability for all resources, power and programs in the church. The pastor is accountable for the effectiveness of its ministry organizations, the training and care of its volunteer and professional workers, for the manner in which it spends its money, etc.

I thought long and hard before writing the following statements regarding the pastor's accountability for I know the tendency of so many pastors to want to control all the ministries of the church, the tendency of so many to believe they must do, or at least somehow be involved in, everything that goes on in the church. Such pastors adopt a benevolent, authoritarian style of ministry which elevates their calling above all others' calling, their ministry above all others' ministry. Jesus said, "It shall not be so among you."

The truth is, the pastor simply cannot do all of the ministries alone. The pastor can block all ministries but cannot carry out all necessary ministries. The pastor who tries is not a church "grower," but is a church "shrinker." Such a pastor will soon find the church shrinking down to the size of his or her own limited ability.

The pastor must learn the skill of delegation; of giving others the freedom and ability to carry out the church's ministries, while retaining primary accountability to Christ for the overall life and ministry of the church. Delegation is a part of the ministry model for the New Testament church, see Mark 6:7-13, 30; Luke 10:1-3,16,17; Matthew 28:16-20.

In his excellent book, *Sojourners Into the Land of Promise*, Chuck Wilson says, "One can read the New Testament and substitute "management" for "stewardship." It will do no harm to the meaning. Indeed it will be enhanced with fuller meaning. For management (organizational leadership) and stewardship, when their best meanings are attributed to them, mean the same thing. To be a good church manager means being an effective steward over the part of the institutional church for which one has been assigned accountability.[2]

When you reflect on your life in God would there not be something lacking if Christ did not offer all three ministries to you? Are there not times when you relate to him as your priest, other times when you relate to him as prophet, and times when you need him to assist you in managing the everyday affairs of your life? And so it is with congregations, but unfortunately many do not have all three ministries being offered with equal care and effectiveness. Far too many church leaders major either on priestly ministry or prophetic, while tending to ignore the managerial ministry as much as possible.

Now we turn our attention to a discussion of why each one of the three ministries are so important.

THE THREE LEVELS OF HUMAN ENCOUNTER

We each live and move and have our being at three levels of human relationships:

INTRAPERSONAL: At this level we experience ourselves as individuals, separate from others, private, unique, different from all others, alone before our creator.

INTERPERSONAL At this level we experience our existence in and through relationships with others. These relationships influence our sense of reality, shape our life and embody our being. Here God speaks to us through others — "Where two or three are gathered together . . . I am in their midst."

SUPRAPERSONAL/PUBLIC: At this level we are aware we exist and live out our lives in institutions, social structures, cultural factors, and the public processes of society around us; business, law, government, education, church, family, etc. We are necessarily a part of these institutions and structures. We cannot be totally private persons and live a full and meaningful life.

28

THE THREE LEVELS OF SPIRITUAL ENCOUNTER

Just as there are three levels of human encounter, so there are three levels of spiritual encounter:

MYSTICAL DIMENSION: This dimension encompasses the invisible and secret encounter we have with God at the interior "core" of our being. It involves our spiritual experience which is cared for through those elements of the faith generally known as "piety"; prayer, meditation, silence/solitude. Our "journey inward" with Christ.

PROPHETIC DIMENSION: This encompasses the encounter we have with God through others. "The word of Christ is often stronger in the heart of our brothers or sisters than it is in our own heart."[3] The prophetic dimension of our spiritual life adds "words" to our mystical experience, so that we, and others, can "hear" what the voice of God is speaking to the "core" of our being.

ACTIVISTIC SERVICE DIMENSION: This encompasses the encounter we have with God through offering our strengths, talents, and intellect to activistic ministries. The activistic dimension embodies our mystical experience, and our prophetic word, in flesh and blood so people can "see" and "touch" our faith. This is faith doing justice, faith offering love in concrete forms, faith emboding truth. Our "journey outward" with Christ.

PUTTING IT ALL TOGETHER

It is now possible to pull all these together to show why Christ continues to call church leaders to the three expressions of ministry within the congregation.

Each person within the congregation, and the congregation itself, lives life at three levels of human encounter	And at three levels of spiritual encounter	Each of which is primarily supported by a particular type of ministry
Intrapersonal Level	Mystical Dimension	Priestly Ministry
Interpersonal Level	Prophetic Dimension	Prophetic Ministry
Suprapersonal/ Public Level	Activistic-Service Dimension	Organizational Leader Ministry

It is vital to remember that the three ministries are not as separate as the chart may suggest. There is overlap. They are interrelated. Each is supported by the others. For example, if the activistic ministries of the church are not influenced and supported by the mystical dimension of the workers, if they do not have an inner core of spiritual power, the workers will soon become tired, lose spirit, begin to quarrel, burn out. The church, itself, will become little more than a second class social service agency with a great deal of activity, but lacking the spirit-power necessary to speak to the deepest needs of persons or to transform the institutions and culture around it.

Jesus knew this very well in his own life and for that reason punctuated his public ministry with seasons of private prayer and meditation. In the hours of secret prayer he gained the strength for his public ministry.

He also knew we would need such a "power base" and for that reason taught that if we wanted to bear fruit we must pay careful attention to our connection with him, John 15:1-8,16. He said, "If you make my word your home, you will be my disciples," John 8:31. de Foucauld says, "If there is no inner life, however great may be the zeal, the high intention, the hard work, no fruit will come forth . . ."[4]

30

On the other hand if the mystical, pietistic experiences of the workers are not personified through activistic service, patterned after Christ's call to action in Matthew 25:31-40 and in Matthew 28:18-20, the church will soon become an island of irrelevancy floating in a sea of tremendous world need, an enclave of persons who have taken the journey inward—and have closed the door behind them. Then prayer disintegrates into "vain repetitions," and persons fall into pietistic narcissism. They sit around counting their many blessings with utter disregard for the "journey outward" which would move them out of their little security systems into the ministries needed to transform societies, institutions and cultural norms.

HOW ARE THE THREE MINISTRIES RELATED, HOW ARE THEY DEPENDENT UPON ONE ANOTHER?

The relationship of the three ministries is both a "building block" effect, and cyclical. Effective priestly ministry is foundational to the people's acceptance of the prophetic word. However, it takes more than priestly ministry to generate the concern and energy necessary to empower a congregation to carry out effective program ministries. The dis-comforting effect of the prophetic word is also necessary.

The message of the priest is "you are loved of God just as you are. You do not have to do anything in order to be loved of God. You are already "special" to him."

The message of the prophet is, "Even though God already loves you just as you are, he does not intend for you to stay just as you are. Whenever the Spirit touches you, he is nudging you to keep moving toward all that God wants you to be and do."

The message of the organization leader is, "In order for any of us to be or do all that God has chosen for us, we must live and work together in Christian community. There are no lone rangers on the road to heaven. We are called to organize ourselves for ministry and for growth."

These are the "building blocks." Until the people feel loved, accepted and affirmed by you, until you are proven in your love and desire to serve them as priest, they will not trust you enough, nor care for you enough to seriously consider the discomforting words you must bring as prophet. Until the people realize themselves to be a forgiven and loved people, until they are at peace within themselves, they will have little interest or energy to offer love, peace and service to others.

When the congregation hears the word of love, forgiveness, and acceptance for itself there is always the temptation to "settle" there. Having now found a place of acceptance, persons set about to preserve things as they are, "We're comfortable here, please don't disturb us, or we may lose our feeling of acceptance and fellowship."

Now the congregation needs a prophet! One to nudge them, to challenge them, to "stir up" the faith that is in danger of being locked up in quiet comfort.

There is a tension between the message of the priest and of the prophet. A kind of unsettling that generates the energy needed to make people willing to answer the nudge of God to commit themselves to active program ministries.

When people are too comfortable they do not want to move in any direction. They stagnate and petrify. But when they are too uncomfortable they become quarrelsome and finally paralyzed. However, when the ministries of priest and prophet are kept in proper tension the people become energized and willing to organize themselves for action.

Whenever the church organizes itself for action against evil in all its forms it quickly finds itself being bruised and spent. Now, as never before, it needs the priest to remind them that they are loved of God, not abandoned. Even in their tiredness they are "special" to God.

But how is one to know when each of the three ministries may be most appropriate and effective? That is the subject of the following chapters. We will deal with the question by first identifying a number of "seasons" or "passages" through which God leads each congregation. After this we will attempt to show which ministry type may be most effective during each "season."

FOOTNOTES: The Three-In-One Ministry to the New Testament Church

1. For a detailed discussion of this responsibility and how to do it, see *Revitalizing the 20th Century Church*, Perry and Shawchuck, Moody Press, 1982.
2. Charles Wilson, *Sojourners in the Land of Promise*, Spiritual Growth Resources, 1981, pp. 11, 12.
3. Dietrich Bonhoeffer, *Life Together*, Harper & Row, 1954.
4. Charles de Foucauld, *Meditations of a Hermit*, trans. by Charlotte Balfour, Orbis, 1981.

This space is reserved for you to jot down your learnings and to add your own thoughts to the chapter.

"The Lord is my shepherd, I shall lack nothing. He makes me lie down in green pastures, he leads me beside quiet waters."

Psalm 23:1,2

"When you pass through the waters, I will be with you; and when you pass through the rivers, they will not sweep over you. When you walk through the fire, you will not be burned; the flames will not set you ablaze. For I am the Lord, your God, the Holy One of Israel, your Savior."

Isaiah 43:2,3a

THE SEASONS OF EXPERIENCE
THROUGH WHICH GOD LEADS THE CHURCH

As the Church, or one of its local congregations, lives out its life it finds itself passing through a number of identifiable conditions. The Church has known this about itself for centuries and has attempted to identify and express its various "conditions" through liturgical colors, symbols, and "seasons."

Each of these seasons can best be responded to by a certain type of ministry. That is to say there are times the church will respond best to a priest, at other times the group needs a prophet, and at other times an organizational leader.

THE SEASONS OF THE CHURCH

Over the centuries the Church has developed liturgical means of identifying and describing the set of experiences which seem inevitably to come to the congregation. The seasons of experience are: Advent, Christmas, Epiphany, Lent, Easter, and Pentecost-Kingdomtide.

THE SEASON OF PREPARATION
AND SEARCH: Advent

Nothing happens in the Church or in the Christian life without the people wanting and expecting something to happen.

The Church has come to understand this, and for this reason begins its year with Advent; the season of expectant preparation and search. Some of the words and themes which describe the meaning of this season are: preparation, expectancy, hope, search.

The first Advent Season came into the humdrum existence of a depressed people. But there came a moment when a shudder passed through the life of those people and they began to make preparation. They felt an expectancy, a hope — and they didn't know what it was for.

We have the advantage of Christian tradition to tell us the meaning of the Advent experience. They didn't. This expectancy came to them and they were unable to know where this search would lead them. But they gave themselves to it and wonderful things began to happen. Shepherds heard a new song in the air, a message they had never heard before, "Peace on Earth, Good Will Toward Men."

And one night a man walked out on his porch, looked up into the sky, and thought he saw a new star. He didn't know where the star came from but it attracted him like a magnet, night after night. At last he had to tell his friends. They looked and agreed that, indeed, it was a new star. We call them the wise men. I wonder what their friends called them when they decided to "hitch their wagon" to a star, not knowing where it would lead them.

And so it was that persons young and old, rich and poor began hoping . . . expecting — and at that moment a little baby was born in a borrowed manger, in the wayside village of Bethlehem. God responded to their deepest longings, but not as they expected.

RESPONSE TO OUR SEARCH: Christmas

God always responds to hopeful expectancy on the part of his people. Whenever a church enters into an Advent Season; begins to search, to expect, to hope, it will soon feel a sort of new pregnancy stirring within it. God comes to expectant people with a gift. Very often, however, the gift is so different from what they expected they do not recognize it.

And so it was with the persons to whom God gave his Grand Christmas Gift. Consider John the Baptist. He had been sent to tell the people to prepare for the Messiah-gift, but the Messiah was so different from what he expected that he lived with him for thirty years and never recognized him. They began their ministries side-by-side and still he did not recognize him. On the day after he baptized Jesus, John was heard to say, "He walked with us and I did not recognize him. I even baptized him, and I still didn't know who he was," John 1:31-33.

John was not expecting the gift to come in such a plain package. Even he could not have guessed that God would give such a gift. "He walked with us and we didn't know who he was." But that's the way it is with God. There is something very surprising, and also very hidden about God and the "Gifts" he wants to give us. Two Scripture verses point to the "hiddenness" of his gifts; "Do not cast your pearls before swine," Matthew 7:6. Jesus is saying here, "we do not reveal the mystery of God's truth to the casual observer. Understanding is reserved for the serious searcher." This is underscored in Jeremiah 29:13, "You will seek me and find me when you search for me with all your heart."

The words and themes which describe the experience of Christmas are: gift, surprise, joy, birth, incarnation.

THE SEASON OF SHARING THE GIFT
WITH OTHERS: Epiphany

Just as sure as Advent leads to Christmas, so Christmas leads to Epiphany. The giving of God's extravagant gift thrusts the church into Epiphany.

The words and themes which describe the season of Epiphany are: light, life, manifestation, call, mission. Christmas always leads to Epiphany.

Epiphany is the church standing in awe at the gift God has given. It touches the gift God has given into its experience, into its arms, and asks, "What in this world are we to do with such a gift?" "Who are we supposed to be now that the gift is given?'' When you get such a gift from God, how do you send an appropriate "thank you" note? The Epiphany experience is the church's effort to find answers to its questions. In its attempt to decide what to write on its "thank you" card, the church moves out into missions, spreading of light, giving the good news to people beyond its own borders, planting of the seed.

It works so hard. It goes everywhere spreading its light and its good news. It shouts to all the world, "See the gift God has given us? Isn't it an amazing gift? We want to share it with you too. Please hold him."

THE SEASON OF BREAKING
AND OF DYING: Lent

After awhile Epiphany leads into Lent, unmistakably, unalterably into Lent. We begin to feel unworthy of such gifts, and unequal to the task. We grow tired from all the good work. We have cared for the world, we have neglected to care for ourselves. When we are tired we easily become discouraged. We begin to withdraw from the work and become introspective.

Some of the words and themes which describe Lent are: denial, loneliness, discouragement, depression, desperation, repentence, suffering, death. It begins with a tiredness that leads to depression. The depression leads to despair. Finally there is alienation, brokenness and death.

The church has worked itself to death. The church has sown all of its seed. Now the seed must lie silently in the ground and rest awhile, getting ready for the great multiplication miracle of harvest. Jesus said, "Unless your seed falls into the ground and dies, it remains only a single seed," John 12:24. We don't understand why God ordained it so. But our inability to understand doesn't change the principle: the doorway to life is death, unless there is a breaking, there can be no multiplying, Mark 6:41.

Unless all the seeds we plant; all our hopes, our efforts, our programs are finally surrendered up to God to the

39

point of death, they will remain a single seed. We may keep it alive but it will never multiply. What a powerful message for leaders and congregations who can allow no program to die, can run no risks, tolerate no failure; who believe that every sign of tiredness and discouragement among the people is the result of sin. The truth is God leads the church through Lent in order to give it new life. Yet how much the church wants to avoid Lent, to the point of going to the garden and praying, "Father, if there is any way to avoid this cup, take it away."

THE SEASON OF RESURRECTION LIFE: Easter

The season of tiredness, despair, alienation and death leads to God's second surprising gift; new life, resurrection life, eternal life. Christmas and Easter are the most creative and playful expressions of God's relationship to the church. What surprise that Christ should be poverty born when everyone expected the Messiah to reign from a throne. What a greater surprise that on the third day the dead seed should erupt into new life.

Just when everyone thought it was all over, just when they were gathering the spices to embalm their dreams, just as they were coming to say their final goodbyes—they discovered that the stone blocking the way to immortality had been rolled away! One thing can be said about God, he doesn't play the game by conventional rules.

Some words and themes which describe the Easter experience are: resurrection, new life, redemption, triumph.

THE SEASON OF HARVEST AND CELEBRATION: Pentecost-Kingdomtide

Close on the heels of the new life experience comes harvest time, ushered in with the power of the Holy Spirit. At Christmas God sends his son saying, "I want to be with you." At Pentecost he sends his Spirit saying, "I want to be with-in you," prompting one Bible writer to say, "God wants to be close to us, closer than our own breath."

Pentecost; a new spirit, a new power working with the

church; dunamis, dynamite, or simply a new ability with which to do its work.

Lent, Easter, Pentecost-Kingdomtide; what a poignant trilogy: the three experiences combining to remind us God's strength indeed is made most evident at the points of our greatest weaknesses.

Kingdomtide is that wonderful season in the experience of a church when all of its harvests come home. It is the "other side" of Epiphany, a time in the experience of a church in which whatever it attempts seems to work, whatever it touches turns to success; when it sees its little seed multiply into sheaves, Psalms 126:6.

But after the harvest is all in there comes a time when the church begins to say, "Our buildings are built, our mortgages all burned, our ministries fruitful beyond our wildest dreams. Now what?" And with that question the church moves forward into Advent and begins its journey through the seasons all over again.

The church or the groups that you lead are at this moment, each one of them, somewhere along the journey of seasons. As you think about it you are probably able, even now, to identify the season your group is passing through.

THE EFFECT OF MINISTERIAL LEADERSHIP UPON THE SEASONS

What I have said about a local church passing through the seasons of Christian experience can also be said about individuals, ministry groups, and entire denominations. I think, for example, there are certain churches that are presently in Kingdomtide; such as the Assemblies of God and the Seventh Day Adventists. These churches are in a season of world-wide multiplication and harvest.

The United Methodist Church, on the other hand, is in Lent. It shows signs of tiredness, discouragement, decline. But it is working its way through the Lenten Season and its Easter is coming soon. Easter for United Methodists may still be five or ten years away but it is coming. Signs are appearing nation-wide. From Maine to California, United Methodists are deciding to live, not die. Archbishop William Temple once said, "It is an unalterable fact of history that when the church is most dead, from out of its very being God raises up new life."

The United Methodist Church has been in Lent since the late 60's. That's a long time to be in Lent. This season was probably unduly extended as a result of the predominate type of ministry in the church from the 60's until now.

Previous to the 1960's the Methodist and the Evangelical United Brethren churches experienced an Epiphany season of twenty or more years. Signs of expansion were everywhere. In the 1950's these churches built an almost unprecedented number of new buildings, expanded hundreds of existing ones, extended missionary action in every part of the world. The clergy led the church, inspired the church with a predominantly prophetic ministry and the general boards provided much by way of organizational skills and resources. These ministry types were well matched for a church in Epiphany.

Then in the late 1960's, the church began showing signs of tiredness and withdrawal. It had worked itself to death. It had planted its seed and needed time to rest a while before harvest.

But the clergy leaders and the general agencies did not recognize this. Instead they increased the fervor of their prophetic ministry. Words of judgment flowed from pulpit, pen, caucus, and office. This only served to reinforce what the people were already feeling; they really were worthless, the church really was abandoned by God — and death set in without a priest to discern, or to explain that on the other side of Lent lay the promise of Easter.

The United Methodist Church, as all others, must go through its Lent, but I think the season could have been greatly shortened had the clergy and agencies realized that a church in Lent needs a priest ministry. It needs one to encourage, to forgive, to heal. It has already heard the prophetic judgment, and it feels it has no future for which to organize.

But now, in the 1980's, the predominant ministry to the United Methodist Church is becoming that of priest. In recent years the Council of Bishops has called for Bible study and spiritual formation at every level of the church. And the church has heard!

Perhaps the lesson to the Assemblies of God, to United Methodists, and *all* others is, "Whatever season you find yourself in, this too, shall pass."

And for certain the lesson I'm trying to teach to you is:

1) Learn how to read "season" signs of your church and its groups, and

2) Learn how to most effectively lead the church during its seasons by matching the three-in-one ministries to the leadership needs of the congregation.

This space is reserved for you to jot down your learnings and to add your own thoughts to the chapter.

"Now, O Lord my God, you have made your servant king in place of my father David. But I am only a little child and do not know how to carry out my duties. Your servant is here among the people you have chosen, a great people, too numerous to count or number. So give your servant a discerning heart to govern your people and to distinguish between right and wrong. For who is able to govern this great people of yours?"

"The Lord was pleased that Solomon had asked for this. So God said to him, 'Since you have asked for this and not for long life or wealth for yourself, nor have asked for death of your enemies but for discernment in administering justice, I will do what you have asked. I will give you a wise and discerning heart, so that there will never have been anyone like you, nor will there ever be.' "

1 Kings 3:7-12

DECIDING WHICH MINISTRY TYPE TO
USE IN EACH SEASON OF EXPERIENCE

The church perhaps never needs just one type of ministry — at least not very long. There is always need for each of the three ministries.

It is also true, however, that each "season" calls for one of the ministries to predominate, to set the tone, and for the other two to support. Many leaders, however, adopt one ministry as their "forte" which they use predominately in every situation or season.

This can, and sometimes does, have serious negative results. For example, a predominately prophetic ministry in a church deep in Lent serves to paralyze the people with guilt and despair. Whereas a predominate priestly ministry to a church in Lent tends to affirm the people, to awaken them to the fact that God loves them just as they are. After a while, hope is born anew in their hearts — and they are on their way out of Lent into Easter.

Let's try a hand at matching the ministries with the Seasons.

SEASON: Advent

MINISTRY TYPE:
> Predominate: Prophet

> Support: Organizational Leader and Priest

RATIONALE:
> Advent comes as a time in the life of a church

when persons begin to feel something new and different is about to happen. The church is awakening to a sense of expectancy. There is hope and excitement. But, as of yet no clear direction is being discerned. There is, however, no doubt that, "God is about to do something good among us."

Now a prophet of hope is needed to encourage the people to give themselves to the search even though they don't know where it may lead them, and to listen carefully to God for a "word" that will begin to clarify the congregation's mission.

The word of the prophet must be supported by the organizational leader who should enable the congregation to carry out an organized "search" for what God is bringing them. This is a wonderful time for such "planning" processes as mission clarification and community discernment — all carried out in the context of quiet prayer and reflection. Advent is a time for organized "pondering," Luke 1:29.

The priest should also be supporting by providing worship opportunities designed to awaken the deepest longings of the people to call forth the cry, "Come! O Come, Thou Long Expected Jesus."

POSSIBLE SERMON/DISCUSSION THEMES:
The "Advent" of Abraham, who started out not knowing where he was going, Hebrews 11:8, 9. The "Advent" of Mary who did not understand the meaning of Gabriel's words but nonetheless kept them in her heart and gave herself completely over to God's disposal, Luke 1:26-38.

SEASON: Christmas

MINISTRY TYPE:
Predominate: Priest

Support: Prophet and Organizational Leader

47

RATIONALE:
Christmas is a wonderful, brief moment of recognition when the church discovers a completely unexpected gift, given in response to its hopeful preparation and search. In this moment the congregation must celebrate, must praise God for the unexpected and undeserved Gift. The priest, of course, leads the celebration.

At the high moment of celebration, the prophet must sound the great commission: Go — make disciples of all nations. Teach them to observe all I have commanded you. Go — feed someone who is hungry. Give water to someone who is thirsty. Be a friend to a stranger. Give a coat to someone who is naked. Take care of the sick. Don't forget those who are in prison, Matthew 28:16-20, 25:31-36.

Christmas is the energizing event which thrusts the congregation forward from the season of preparation (Advent) into the season of call and ministry (Epiphany).

POSSIBLE SERMON/DISCUSSION THEMES:
God is with Us, Isaiah 40:28-31, Matthew 1:22, 23. What "treasure" have you to give him, Matthew 2:11. Where in your life is Jesus being "born" just now, what does the "manager" symbolize in your life, Luke 2:6, 7.

SEASON: Epiphany

MINISTRY TYPE:
Predominate: Organizational Leader

Support: Priest and Prophet

RATIONALE:
There are those times in the life of every church when the congregation is ready; not so much to be ministered unto, but to minister to others. This is the Epiphany moment.

48

It is the time when people begin to say, "We are ready to go! And we will go! But *how* do we go, and to *whom*?" The answers to these questions presuppose there will be organization and leadership for ministry. This is a time for congregational self-assessment, for ministry program planning, for implementation, evaluation, and for conflict management. Epiphany is always a time of much conflict over goals and methods, see Acts 11 and 15.

The organizational leader provides for the planning and implementation of ministry, the recruitment and training of volunteer workers, and the necessary resources to carry out the ministries.

The book of Acts is a story of the Church's first Epiphany. The early Christians were so overwhelmed by the realization of God's gift to them they couldn't help but enter Epiphany, "For we *cannot* stop speaking what we have seen and heard," Acts 4:20. So they scattered everywhere — and everywhere they went they gave witness to the Gift, Acts 8:4.

In seasons of much work it's altogether too easy for the congregation to take its eyes off the Gift, to forget for *whom* it is expending itself, and *why*. So the priest must often call the people together to rehearse the story of how the Gift was given to them, and to invite them to rest awhile to renew their strength for the labor, Isaiah 40:28-31.

The prophet is there to urge them to more labor, for this is planting time and it will not last forever, John 9:4.

POSSIBLE SERMON/DISCUSSION THEMES:
Almost anything from Acts. Luke 4:18-21. "God is working with us," Hag. 2:4; Mark 16:20; I Cor. 3:9. "Finish what you have begun," Neh. 6:3; Zec. 4:9; Luke 9:62.

The entire book of Nehemiah is an Epiphany book showing the organizational leader at work. First, Nehemiah *clarified his mission*, Ch. 2:2-6. Next, he *took an assessment* of the work situation, Ch. 2:11-16. Then he *recruited others* to help him *plan* and *carry out* the work,

Ch. 2:16-18. Finally, he *implemented* the plan, Ch. 3.
Nehemiah set a model for every organizational leader to
follow a model of action interspersed with prayer. Prayer
was integral to his leadership.

SEASON: Lent

MINISTRY TYPE:
Predominate: Priest

Support: Prophet and Organizational Leader

RATIONALE:
The congregation cannot give its undivided attention to services and programs indefinitely, for in the
course of time persons become tired, lose a sense of the
meaning and purpose of it all, and almost without notice
slip into a season of Lent.

All of nature needs its times of aloneness and rest. The
Old Testament prescribed every seventh year as a
"Lenten" Sabbath; a year of rest. That might still be a
good model for the church today.

Lent is experienced as a time when the people aren't interested in adding new program outreach ministries, planning and training sessions are poorly attended. The congregation turns its attention inward upon itself. Lent finds
the people wanting to deepen their own inner spiritual life.
They want times of solitude and prayer.

Persons are wanting to deal with the "dark" side of
their lives, but in order to face the dark side they must
know that God loves them just as they are, that they are a
gifted and a special people even though they don't feel
gifted or special. And they must know there is forgiveness
for whatever their probing into the darkness may reveal.
This is why the ministry of priest is of paramount importance in the Lenten times. God calls to the priest: Comfort, O comfort my people. Speak kindly to them. Tell
them their war is ended, their sin removed, Isaiah 40:1, 2.

Lent is also a season of much conflict in the church, but of a different nature than Epiphany conflicts. Lenten conflicts are often conflicts of values, as persons begin to question the meaning of their faith. Other Lenten conflicts are interpersonal quarrels over almost insignificant things. When persons are not feeling good about themselves deep down inside, they tend to "take it out" on others around them.

As these signs increase the priest must also increase affirmation, love, forgiveness. The gentleness of the priest must be supported by the powerful word of the prophet, and it must consistently be a word of hope, not judgment; of the visitation of God, not separation.

All churches must go through seasons of Lent, but most are kept there for longer than they need be simply because the pastor reinforces negative feelings and spiritual numbness by speaking words of judgment. Lent is also extended because the leaders do not know how to manage the many conflicts that surface during Lent. The result being that persons pull farther apart into cold cells of isolation and bitter loneliness.

In Scripture, we have a sad picture of the types of behavior many leaders display when their church enters a Lenten season, it is the picture of the disciples during Jesus' season of Lent:

1) They didn't understand what was going on, and were unaware of what type of ministry would have been most helpful, so they slept, Matthew 26:36-46.

2) They got caught up in the conflicts that were breaking out, Matthew 26:50-52.

3) They finally resigned their position and fled the scene, Matthew 26:69-74.

POSSIBLE SERMON/DISCUSSION THEMES:

Almost anything from (Second) Isaiah, chapters 40-66. These chapters were spoken to a people deep in their Lenten season. A careful reading will tell you what to preach to a church in Lent, i.e., 41:1, 6, 9-10; 42:3, 6; 43:1-13; 46:3-4.

Luke is a New Testament prophet of unconditional love and hope. He follows in the footsteps of Isaiah. Almost any of his stores are appropriate; i.e., Zaccheus 19:1-10, prodigal son 15:11-32; Road to Emmaus 24:13-31.

SEASON: Easter

MINISTRY TYPE:
> Predominate: Priest

> Support: Prophet and Organizational Leader

RATIONALE:
> Lent wears on. Then without announcement, without planning or organizing, new life explodes into being, the church experiences Resurrection.

The message has gotten through! The people have heard they are loved of God. Suddenly the body shudders into new life. The seeds sewn in Epiphany, having rested during Lent, now erupt into life.

Only the priest is needed here. This moment calls for celebration. One cannot plan for, or organize Easter. One shouldn't try to defend Easter. One should merely respond to it with great appreciation and celebration. The only offering that makes any sense at Easter is the offering of one's whole self, an offering of the entire church for the Kingdomtide Season which is soon to follow.

SEASON: Pentecost - Kingdomtide

MINISTRY TYPE:
> Predominate: Organizational Leader

> Support: Prophet and Priest

RATIONALE:
> This is a time when the church experiences

power beyond its own ability, a relative ease in focusing its efforts, a sense of confidence and competence in its ministry and a great sense of fulfillment in all it does. The church feels called, empowered, enabled.

It is a time when all of the ministries carried out by the congregation, all of the seeds shown in Epiphany, bear their fruit for the kingdom. It is harvest time, and there is much work to be done. Jesus is urging, "Lift up your eyes, Look at the fields, They are ready for harvest."

Now the organizational leader must come to the front. There are plans to be made. Someone must manage the inevitable conflicts over methods. New members must be assimilated and discipled or they will be lost. There is a need to recruit and train more volunteers, to hire more staff. Perhaps a new building is needed.

And in all of this there is not a moment to lose. Kingdomtide never lasts "long enough." There will come a time, whether soon or late, when the season is past. The priest can help keep the moment alive by receiving the harvest offerings with great celebration.

When the season is past, the prophet sounds the word that leads the congregation into a new cycle of seasons. "Look"! he says, "Is that a new star I see up there? Listen! is that a new song I hear?" Once again the people begin to sense a new excitement in the air — Advent has begun!

POSSIBLE SERMON/DISCUSSION THEMES:
God multiplies our efforts, Joel 2:21-27, Spirit power for our ministry, Acts 1:8, 2:1-4, and 41-47.

53

This space is reserved for you to jot down your learnings and to add your own thoughts to the chapter.

"It was he who gave some to be apostles, some to be prophets, some to be evangelists, and some to be pastors and teachers, to prepare God's people for works of service, so that the body of Christ may be built up until we all reach unity in the faith and in the knowledge of the Son of God and become mature, attaining to the whole measure of the fullness of Christ."

"Then we will no longer be infants, tossed back and forth by the waves, and blown here and there by every wind of teaching and by the cunning and craftiness of men in their deceitful scheming. Instead, speaking the truth in love, we will in all things grow up into him who is the Head, that is, Christ. From him the whole body, joined and held together by every supporting ligament, grows and builds itself up in love, as each part does its work."

Ephesians 4:11-16

"So the twelve gathered all the disciples together and said, 'It would not be right for us to neglect the ministry of the word of God in order to wait on tables. Brothers, choose seven men from among you who are known to be full of the Spirit and wisdom. We will turn this responsibility over to them and will give our attention to prayer and the ministry of the word.' "

"This proposal pleased the whole group. They chose Stephen, a man full of faith and of the Holy Spirit; also Philip, Procorus, Nicanor, Timon, Parmenas, and Nicolas from Antioch, a convert to Judaism. They presented these men to the apostles, who prayed and laid their hands on them."

"So the word of God spread. The number of disciples in Jerusalem increased rapidly, and a large number of priests became obedient to the faith."

Acts 6:2-7

55

THE EFFECTS OF ORGANIZATIONAL LEADERSHIP UPON THE GROWTH AND MINISTRY OF THE CHURCH

The best preaching and/or counseling cannot soften the negative effects of ineffective organizational leadership in the congregation.

In recent years a number of extensive studies have been done into the factors which foster congregational revitalization. In each of these studies the leadership style of the pastor has been rated of extreme importance. Few pastors seem to realize this, however, and want to believe that they can build a great church simply upon the basis of their preaching. I doubt this ever was the case. It most certainly isn't true today.

Good preaching *is* important. Sensitive priestly ministry *is* important — but these are not enough to build a strong congregation. Preaching must be supported by effective program ministries. If this is not the case the preaching will be crippled.

In the early 1970's I directed an action-research project designed to develop a theory and a practice of congregational renewal. We worked closely with forty Protestant and Catholic parishes.

You may recall the late 1960's and early 1970's; the social revolution, the endless Vietnam War, Watergate, assassinations of leaders. These were days of unpresidented distrust of all leaders. Leaders were held in distrust simply because they were leaders.

Yet in our research among the parishes in our project the laity consistently reported the number one factor influencing positive change was the leadership style of the pastor. Every parish reporting a new spirit and vitality was pastored by a person who was: 1) able to communicate love and affirmation to the congregation; that is, the pastor was effective in the priestly office; and 2) was able to adapt flexible leadership styles based upon the needs of the various parish organizations.

Conversely, the laity in every parish showing a decline in vitality reported 1) the pastor was unaffirming and caustic in the priestly office; and 2) consistently operated out of an authoritarian style of leadership.

I have thought much about these findings and have used them as a filter through which to observe the effectiveness of pastors. It is my opinion that the pastor's acceptance as prophet or effectiveness as organizational leader depends upon a proven priestly ministry. To become truly prophetic within the congregation requires first that the people love and trust you. They must know that even when you pronounce judgment you love them enough to stand in their stead before God, in their place at judgment. If they do not trust you, if they do not feel you deeply love them, they will "tune out" your prophetic message, vote you out, ask the bishop for a new pastor, or by some other means keep your prophetic word from penetrating their consciousness.

I also observe that lay and clergy leaders who are effective as priests and prophets will soon have people gathering around who are free of the intrapersonal blockages which have cut them off from a sense of the love of God. These persons will now be open to receiving the "meat" of the word, and energized by the spirit to act on it.

If these leaders know how to organize volunteer ministries, plan programs, train workers, manage conflict, the people will throw themselves into the ministry of the church with gusto! It is this type of ministry that transforms persons, congregations and communities. The members of today's Church will, indeed they desperately want to, follow a church leader who has first served them as priest and prophet.

God knows all of this. That is why he provides a three-in-one ministry for the church. Without any one of the ministries in place, the spirit and program will be crippled, the congregation will suffer, and the kingdom of God will languish in your parish.

ORGANIZATIONAL LEADERSHIP THAT TRANSFORMS INSTITUTIONS AND PERSONS

Scripture's call to Christian men and women is to be transformed, Romans 12:1, 2; and to transform the world, Matthew 28:19, 20. This work, while being spiritual, requires organization. Without organization the church cannot carry out its ministries or respond to its Great Commission. Every church organization depends upon effective leadership to be successful.

In his Roman letter, Paul declares the utter dependency of the Great Commission upon organization, "For whoever will call upon the name of the Lord will be saved.
But - how shall they call upon him in whom they have not believed?
And - how shall they believe in him whom they have not heard?
And - how shall they hear without a preacher?
And - how shall they preach unless they are sent?
Romans 10:11-14

Prophets cannot be sent without some form of organization to send them, and the organization cannot function without effective leadership. Prophetic ministry is dependent upon the ministry of the organizational leader, as is the ministry of the priest.

The early apostles knew this and gave themselves to the three ministries. And when the job became too big for them to do alone, they recruited members from the congregation to assume responsibility for many important ministries.

The ministry of the early Church would have been crippled had the apostles said, "God has called us to the priestly and prophetic ministry, we are not interested in the ministry of organizational leadership." As a matter of fact they did think this for awhile. They thought they could give this responsibility away to others, but they soon got over that idea and accepted the three-in-one ministry to which Christ had called them.

Peter urged Paul to see his ministry of organizational leader to be as important as his prophetic preaching, Galatians 2:10. Paul learned this lesson well. At times we see Paul moving across the country as the missionary (prophet and priest), at other times he is the organizational leader, putting together organizations to collect money for the poor Christians in Jerusalem, II Corinthians 8; meeting with Peter and others to manage organizational conflict which has arisen regarding priestly matters, Acts 11 and 15.

Now let's look a bit more closely at Paul's ministry to the Corinthians to see how he uses the three ministry types to motivate people for ministry.

THE TWO INGREDIENTS NECESSARY TO FOSTER A CONGREGATION'S MOTIVATION FOR MINISTRY: Readiness Plus Ability

II Corinthians 8 finds the apostle Paul moving into the ministry of organizational leader. An interesting chain of events has happened in the church at Corinth which has caused Paul to shift emphasis from one office of ministry to another, until he has finally exercised all three ministries. The story actually begins with the first letter to the Corinthians. Paul's first letter begins with the fire and judgment of a prophet. Remember, the prophet convinces of sin, announces judgment, discomforts the people. How comfortable do you suppose the Corinthians were when they read his words, "And I could not speak with you as to spiritual men, but as to men of flesh," 3:1.

This was the church which was so proud of the many spiritual gifts exercised within it. The church which thought itself super-spiritual. A little later he fires another volley at their spiritual pride: "It is actually reported that there is immorality among you of such a kind as does not exist even among the Gentiles," 5:1. He was saying the Gentiles were more moral than they. That must have made some squirm in discomfort.

But the prophet is only getting warmed up, now he is ready to pronounce judgement: "I have already judged him who has committed this . . . (and) I have decided to deliver such a one to Satan for the destruction of his flesh that his spirit may be saved," 5:3-5.

With the word of judgment pronounced upon their sin of spiritual pride and immortality, the prophet continues throughout his first letter with words of instruction; hard but necessary words. I wonder how these people, all so proud of their spiritual gifts and yet so bitter and quarrelsome, must have felt when Paul said:

"If I speak with the tongues of men and of angels, but have not love, I am nothing but a noisy gong or a clanging cymbal. And if I have the gift of prophesy, and know all mysteries and all knowledge; and if I have all faith, so as to remove mountains, but do not have love, I am nothing. And though I give all my goods to feed the poor, and though I give my body to be burned, and have not love, it profits me nothing."

13:1-3

Even though he was using the pronoun "I," they knew he meant "you."

Why did they put up with this? Why did they not simply throw the letter away and send a delegation to stone him? Because Paul had first ministered to them as priest. He had earlier proven his love for them, had heard their prayers of confessions, had planted the church in Corinth.

Now, notice the change, the complete difference in words, tone and style between the first letter and the second. In noticing the difference you will be observing Paul lay aside his ministry-as-prophet to once again take up his ministry-as-priest. II Corinthians 1-7 are the words of a priest.

In the first letter Paul-as-prophet demands they expel a certain member because of his sin, "I have decided to deliver him to Satan," he says. But now he writes to say: Remember my earlier letter to you?

It was out of much affliction and anguish of heart I wrote to you with my tears; not that you should be made sorrowful, but that you might know the love I have especially for you . . . This man has endured sufficient punishment . . . Now I want you to forgive and comfort him . . . I urge you, reaffirm your love for him." 2:4-8.

What a profound charge in Paul's position! These are the words of Paul-as-priest; words meant to forgive, to heal, to carry away all sorrow, to comfort the people.

The congregation is now free of its terrible sin of spiritual pride and of immorality. A new energy and motivation has been given. The congregation is once again READY, and WILLING to organize itself for ministry. So in chapter 8 of II Corinthians, Paul-as-organizational leader begins to organize them for a program to feed the poor. He appoints Titus to be in charge of the program, appoints another to audit the collections, and establishes a time table.

He is organizing them because he knows his ministry as priest and as prophet has created a READINESS to do ministry, but this readiness will soon fade into apathy if he does not create a plan whereby they will be able to act, v. 11.

READINESS and ABILITY. These are the two ingredients necessary for ministry.

Effective priestly and prophetic ministry creates WILLINGNESS to minister. Effective organizational leadership gives persons the ABILITY to do it. This is the way persons come to know Christ, and continue on to serve him. Persons who are provided only a priestly ministry soon become too comfortable, too concerned only about themselves.

Persons need the challenge of the prophet to keep them from snuggling down into their warm experience and falling asleep. When the challenge of the prophet falls upon the ears of a congregation whose own sins are forgiven, whose own prisons are broken, it ignites a readiness to meet the challenge with organized effort.

An organizational leader is then needed to help them match their readiness with ability. Of such a church the Bible testifies: And the gates of hell shall not be able to stand against it.

Of course, nothing to do with human nature is ever so compartmentalized as I am writing about it. A group is probably never 100 percent ready and able, or 100 percent unready and unable. There are always degrees of both present in every congregation. Nonetheless, there are clearly those times when the church is much more ready and able, and there are those times when the church is much less ready and able. In this chapter I have attempted to show that a skillful balance of the three ministries will greatly increase the congregation's readiness and ability to carry out its important ministry. An imbalance of the three will dampen motivation for ministry.

This space is reserved for you to jot down your learnings and to add your own thoughts to the chapter.

"If any of you lacks wisdom, he should ask God, who gives generously to all without finding fault, and it will be given to him. But when he asks, he must believe and not doubt, because he who doubts is like a wave of the sea, blown and tossed by the wind. That man should not think he will receive anything from the Lord; he is a double-minded man, unstable in all he does."

James 1:5-8

"Who is wise and understanding among you? Let him show it by his good life, by deeds done in the humility that comes from wisdom. But if you harbor bitter envy and selfish ambition in your hearts, do not boast about it or deny the truth. Such 'wisdom' does not come down from heaven but is earthly, unspiritual, of the devil. For where you have envy and selfish ambition, there you find disorder and every evil practice.

But the wisdom that comes from heaven is first of all pure; then peace loving, considerate, submissive, full of mercy and good fruit, impartial and sincere. Peacemakers who sow in peace raise a harvest of righteousness."

James 3:13-18

CONCLUSION

In this study we have considered three topics from a biblical and theological perspective.
1. Appropriate ministry styles for the church.
2. The "seasons" of experience which come to a congregation during its faith journey, and
3. The necessity of adapting one's ministry style to facilitate the continued life and growth of the congregation through its seasons of experience.

There are now some important items I want to highlight:
1. A congregation is probably never totally "in" any one season. Congregational life is not static, and not as tidy as my writing may suggest. At anyone time you may find indications of two or three "seasons" within the congregation. Nonetheless, one will predominate.
2. The seasons of the congregation are usually not as cyclical as I have written. For example, the church may journey between Kingdomtide — Advent — Epiphany several times before settling into Lent. But no church can avoid Lent indefinitely. Sooner or later it must be brought back to itself, it must experience suffering or it will lose its sense of the power of Resurrection, Phil. 3:10.
3. The cycle of seasons also holds true for the journey individuals make. For example, we see several of the seasons in Elijah's story. When we are introduced to Elijah, I Kings 17 and 18, he is in Epiphany, having come from his time of preparation (Advent) in the mountains. In Kings 19:1-4, we see him grow tired from all his work and tumble head-long into Lent.

But God sends an angel to "resurrect" him, Ch. 19:5-13. He goes from this Easter experience into a season of Pentecost-Kingdomtide, and finally is caught up by a whirlwind into heaven, I Kings 19:15 - II Kings 2:11.

If the Lord led the great Elijah through such "Seasons," we can safely assume we will also be so led. It is important to remember this in our work with persons who come to us for help in understanding where they are on their own spiritual journey.

POSTSCRIPT

You may be reading this book as part of a larger study, *How To Be A More Effective Church Leader* . If so, I want to turn your attention now to deal specifically with one of the ministry types, that of organizational leader. The study will:

1. Acquaint you with a number of organizational leadership styles and help you identify which ones you are presently using.
2. Teach you how to "read" group situations to determine which leadership style should be most effective.
3. Teach you how to adapt your leadership style to the changing needs of the group to more consistently foster growth and motivation for ministry.

As you can see, the study will lead you to some profoundly important self-discoveries about your important ministry as an organizational leader.

This space is reserved for you to jot down your learnings
and to add your own thoughts to the chapter.

BIBLIOGRAPHY

The following materials are what I would consider "must" reading for expanding your thinking on the subjects covered in this book.

1. *How To Be A More Effective Church Leader,* Norman Shawchuck, Spiritual Growth Resources, Leith, North Dakota, 1981.

   A self-study learning system, focusing upon your ministry as organizational leader; gives you skill in adapting your leadership style to fit the needs of the groups with whom you work.

2. *The Wounded Healer,* Henri J.M. Nouwen, Image Books, New York, 1979.

   The most beautiful and powerful book I have ever read on the pastor-as-priest.

3. *The Good Shepherd: Meditations on Christian Ministry in Today's World,* Lesslie Newbigin, Eerdmans Publishing Co., 1977.

   A series of meditations on ministry dealing with each of the ministry types discussed in this book.

4. *Servant Leadership,* Robert Greenleaf, Paulist Press, 1977 (especially chapters 1,2,7,8,11,12).

   If you read only one book on leadership in your life, this probably should be the one.

5. *A Guide to Prayer for Ministers and Other Servants,* Rueben Job and Norman Shawchuck, The Upper Room, Nashville, 1983.

A daily guide to prayer and meditation for all ministers. Guides ministers on their spiritual journeys by presenting one theme for reflection each week. Includes scriptures, reflective readings, personal retreat designs and much more. This resource is prepared to feed the "priest," "prophet," and "organizational leader" ministries.

A PRAYER FOR MINISTRY

Lord Jesus, it is thine office
    which I hold,
It is thy work I am doing,
It is your people whom
I would build up
It is thy glory that I seek.

Help me, therefore, in this hour,
    that I, poor sinner,
May do and perform it all
    according to thy Holy Will.

Amen.

by G.C. Dieffenbach

ABOUT THE AUTHOR...

Dr. Norman Shawchuck is the president of Shawchuck and Associates, Ltd., specializing in management consulting to religious organizations nationally and internationally; conducting research into religious organizations; and offering training seminars in leadership, conflict management, marketing and spiritual formation.

Dr. Shawchuck is the author/co-author of several books on church leadership and spiritual formation including; *Managing the Congregation: Building Effective Systems to Serve People, Benchmarks of Quality in the Church: 21 Ways to Continuously Improve the Content of Your Ministry, Leading the Congregations: Caring for Yourself While Serving the People, A Guide to Prayer For All God's People, A Guide to Prayer For Ministers and Other Servants, Marketing for the Church: Choosing to Serve People More Effectively, How to Conduct a Spiritual Life Retreat, How To Be A More Effective Church Leader, What it Means To Be A Church Leader, How To Manage Conflict In The Church, Management For Your Church, Let My People Go; Empowering Laity For Ministry and Revitalizing the 20th Century Church.* He is a contributing editor for Leadership; *A Practical Journal For Church Leaders.* He has authored scores of articles and research papers.

Dr. Shawchuck served on the doctoral faculty of McCormick Theological Seminary for many years. He presently is on the doctoral faculties at Trinity Evangelical Divinity School and Asbury Theological Seminary, where he teaches in the fields of religious leadership and spirituality. He is a Research Scholar on the faculty of the school of Industrial Engineering, Northwestern University.